Super Cats Rule

THE BOOKSTORE CAT'S GUIDE TO THE CARE & TRAINING OF HUMANS

Neal Bowers
With drawings by Rose Shipes

Copyright © 2009 Neal Bowers
All rights reserved.

ISBN:1-4392-2221-5
ISBN-13:9781439222218

Visit www.booksurge.com to order additional copies.

"When you see a human weeping,
you can't tell if her heart or her
favorite china cup has been broken."
—Imogene (circa 1850)

"Time is the universal language
of humans, even though it is
meaningless."
—Pablo (1955—1963)

"Only humans <u>work themselves to death</u>
for a <u>better life</u>."
—Henry (1899—1918)

Contents

Preface 1

Chapter 1: Adopting a Human 11

    A. Types of Humans 15
    B. More Than One Human 22
    C. Human Children 26
    D. Other Creatures in the Family 29

Chapter 2: Some Common Misconceptions About Humans 35

    A. Humans Are Untrainable 37
    B. Humans Are Entirely Self-Centered 41
    C. Humans Are High Maintenance 43
    D. Humans Are Intolerant 47

Chapter 3: The Habits of Humans 51

    A. The Curious Human Work Impulse 55
    B. The Odd Play Habits of Humans 59
    C. The Human Diet 62
    D. Human Sleep Patterns 65

Chapter 4: Human Habitats 69

    A. Urban Dwellings 75
    B. Suburban Homes 78
    C. Life in the Country 80
    D. The Vagabond Life 83

Chapter 5: Human Grooming and Toilet Habits 87

    A. Bathing 88
    B. Grooming and Dressing 90
    C. Reflections on Mirrors 94
    D. Toilet Habits. 96

Chapter 6: Human Mating Habits. 99

    A. Sex and the Single Man 101
    B. Sex and the Single Woman. 104
    C. Men and Women Together 107
    D. The Human Dilemma 109

Chapter 7: Some Common Human Ailments . . 111

    A. Diseases That Are Not Species Specific 114
    B. Bad Habits. 117
    C. Serious Substance Abuse 118
    D. Mental and Emotional Health Issues . . 121

Chapter 8: Human Aging and Dying 125

    A. The Myth of Time 129
    B. Life Expectancy and Mortality 131
    C. Faith and Religion 133
    D. Body and Soul 135

Afterword 139

Preface

My name is Eliot, and I live at the local bookstore. The manager found me five-lives-dead in a patch of weeds near the back loading dock.

I have no idea how old I was—fairly young, I suppose, even by human standards. Perhaps someone dumped me there or I wandered for days after a storm or a dog or my own curiosity separated me from my mother and however many brothers and sisters I had.

Anyhow, the manager took me inside and kept me a secret for almost a week, giving me laps of milk from the cap of a prescription bottle and holding me close in a storage room. I don't know why he didn't take me home with him, though it's easy to imagine a wife with allergies or a Doberman in the living room.

He named me Eliot in honor of his favorite poet, a serious man who knew a thing or two about cats. At the time, he didn't know if I was male or female but figured he could call me Elly if necessary. Turned out I was a Tom, just like my namesake—for a while, anyhow.

When other workers found out about me, I was no longer a secret. Even some of the patrons sneaked into the back room to pet me. At first, the manager said they should phone the shelter and have me put up for adoption, because the store's owners would never allow a cat on the premises. But I clung to his shirt and purred so hard that he changed his mind and said the owners didn't have to know. One of the sales clerks said nothing made more sense together than cats and books, and that was that.

I don't know how long ago that was, but since then I've had the run of the place. Sometimes I pretend I'm mousing, just in case the manager expects me to earn my keep; but mostly I lounge about, moving from one sunny spot to another.

People are generally very nice to me, and I don't mind making new friends, though sometimes I get tired of all the attention and hide out in the

"History" section because it gets less traffic than "Self Improvement" or "True Crime." Lately, I've been dozing in a nook between volumes on Marie Antoinette and the Middle Ages. I'm a good-sized cat, but I can still scrooch into fairly tight places. Now and then, a lost and lonely browser running his fingers along the lined up spines gets a jolt when he touches something soft.

I became interested in books as more than a hiding place when I started listening to readings by visiting authors. Curled up just out of view, I could hear each word without becoming a distraction. But I soon grew hungry for something more challenging than listening and learned to peek over people's shoulders as they browsed cook books and biographies and, rarely, even a volume or two of poetry.

To my amazement, I could read faster than any person. Each page came to me as quick as a scent, and I knew instantly what it was saying. I'm not sure I can explain this phenomenon, except to say that a sparrow is not just a sparrow. Its presence marks the air in a way as distinctive as a signature. The same is true for mice and shrews and chipmunks. Each is unique, and since a cat can read each one's name, signed in fear or bravado, stalking prey is an extremely personal thing.

Let's just say that I learned over the years how to stalk books, scenting out each one just by sniffing its spine. In this way, I've read every volume in the store—except for anthologies, which are such a mixture of identities they send me into fits of sneezing.

Whether or not other cats can read in this fashion is something I don't know for sure. Maybe I'm different because I've spent my life among books. It's possible that my senses were altered and refined by my environment. To be honest, I don't feel particularly special. However, just in case I am, I should probably put my talent to good use. And that's where this book comes into the picture.

Of all the books in the store, the ones that disappoint me most are those dealing with cats. It's not that the authors lack good intentions or have nothing useful to say but that they see everything from a human point of view. They write about cat ownership (a notion that makes me snort), cat grooming, feeding, and training (another snort), as if the cat has no say in any of these matters.

Clearly, there's a great need for a book by a cat on all the issues pertaining to the cat's life among humans. That's the space into which I thrust this slender volume, thinking of it as a guide for cats but hoping that humans might also benefit from reading it. Any person who reads this book with a cat in the room should assume that the cat has already apprehended every word and nuance.

Finally, I must say a few words about the composition process that resulted in this book. While reading comes easily to me, writing is another matter entirely. Even though I'm quick with my paws, I'm not much good at the keyboard. However hard I try, things come out spattered with \\\;;]=%##**########. Sometimes it's worse than that. But even if I were an expert typist, it wouldn't be easy to translate scent into sense.

So I had to admit that I needed a human collaborator. My first choice was the store manager who found me, but he was always so busy I couldn't hold his attention. Eventually, I chose a regular book store patron, a writer who writes by longhand on yellow legal pads. He has a few out-of-print volumes in the Local Authors section, and frequently falls asleep in one of the oversized chairs in a rear corner of the store while working on one of his manuscripts.

He often lets me sit on his lap and pets me absentmindedly as he doodles while waiting for ideas to come. So it was easy to climb onto his chest when he dozed off. I got as close to his face as possible and matched our breathing patterns so that he inhaled each time I exhaled. In this way, I was able to inspire him, though I'm sure some people passing by worried that I was stealing his breath. It's funny how often humans get things exactly backwards.

In order for any transfer of knowledge to occur, the human must be in a receptive mode. The person I chose was ideal because he was not simply passively receptive but fell asleep wishing for some great, new insight. You might say he was doubly ready for what I had to impart.

When he awoke and began to process everything I had given him, he naturally believed the thoughts and ideas were his own. Even these words that explain how he came to have a cat's view of humans are for him part of his own narrative creation. No matter how much I insist that I am the true author, his name on the cover of this book says otherwise.

This is how it has been for cats from the beginning. Da Vinci paints an enigmatic smile, and no one notices how cat-like it is. Newton falls asleep under an apple tree while petting a yellow cat but all anyone remembers is the apple. That omission bothers me more than many because it's so obvious that no one understands gravity better than a cat.

If we sometimes seem aloof and act superior, it's because of what we know about our role in human history. Sadly, no despot has ever liked cats, and that circumstance has kept us from shaping the world in an even better fashion. Still, we've done our best, and in my own small way I hope to make a contribution with this little book.

Chapter 1
Adopting a Human

People acquire things; cats acquire people.

Despite what you may have heard, humans aren't all bad. In fact, many can be properly conditioned and trained to make excellent companions. What they lack in grace they make up for in body heat, which is at least a small compensation for their cumbersome size.

Of course, not every cat needs a human. If you're feral, for instance, you know in advance that a feline/human relationship isn't going to work out. You'll find domestic life intolerable, and your human's efforts to relate to you will feel like a suffocating need.

Similar problems arise for the solitary cat who prefers a home and regular meals but doesn't want to be petted and loathes the "oogy-googy" baby treatment. If groping hands and expressions like "tum here iddle snookums" make you want to hack up a hair-ball, maybe the hobo life is best for you.

However, there are cats who couldn't survive outside a human home. If you're a purebred anything, life in the open is not for you—too many burrs for your silky fur, too little time for self-admiration. And any cat who has spent a day or two in the rough yards of the neighborhood will tell you that free-range food is overrated.

I've heard of a Persian who escaped and remained at large for three weeks, despite having her picture posted on every light pole in town. She survived on scraps foraged from garbage cans and whatever mangled things the crows called to her attention. In the end, she surrendered at her old back door, weary of freedom and ready once more to adore the sound of a can opener.

What humans don't know is how much they need us. Most of the great ideas that have shaped human history were inspired by cats. Even the little notions that make a tiny difference were passed along in exactly the way I inspired this writer in the bookstore.

Humans also don't know how the adoption process really works. One of us may show up mewing at a door after days of checking out all the prospects in the neighborhood, but the human will think she has chosen when she takes the waif inside. In my own case, I'm certain I gave out a weak cry from my weed patch so I could adopt the bookstore manager and then the entire staff.

At pet stores and animal shelters, each cat learns quickly how to attract or repel various prospects. A sneeze or two will send a clumsy-handed

teenager to the next cage, and watery eyes will make the over-demanding kind move along. If you are unable to sneeze or tear-up at will, your best ploy is lethargy. Make yourself limp and non-responsive to the overtures of all the wrong ones.

Resist all temptation to scratch or bite, because that kind of behavior will limit your access to other humans and greatly lessen your chance of finding a person to call your own. While you don't want to select just anyone who comes along, you definitely don't want to reduce the pool of available candidates.

A. Types of Humans 🐾

Humans come in a few basic colors, though the most pronounced differences aren't a matter of color at all. In fact, black and white fall easily within our range of perception because we see primarily in shades of gray. As far as we're concerned, some people are simply more sharply defined than others. Blue, red, or yellow makes a difference to us only along a scale of gray. So color is never an issue when choosing a human for adoption.

Gender probably shouldn't matter, but it's historically true that female humans are more inclined to be cat lovers than is the male of the species. This odd difference has something to do with social conditioning. The female is more likely to feel at ease displaying her emotions and affections.

The male, on the other paw, tends to conceal his feelings with a display of indifference or even gruffness.

Hormones may also play a role, causing males to behave more aggressively, especially in the presence of other males. It's not uncommon to hear a group of men talking about cats in the most demeaning way. In fact, most of the bad traits attributed to cats (such as aloofness, sneakiness, and narcissism) originated in the talk of men.

Despite this fundamental difference, no cat should automatically eliminate men from adoption, because there are exceptions to the gender rule. Men who are more secure in their identities are more likely to appreciate cats. And even those with borderline insecurities can make excellent adoptees, though they tend to keep their feline associations a secret from their male co-workers and from most of their male friends.

Some cats are naturally drawn to hardship cases—men who hunt, talk about trucks, and brag about their sexual exploits. If you feel attracted to this type, make certain you fully understand the difficulties before proceeding with the adoption. Changing this kind of man is unlikely, and the best you can hope for is a kind of split personality. You will be admired only in private and never introduced to any of your adoptee's friends. Sometimes, you may be locked away in a bedroom or closet where you will overhear your adoptee engaging with other men in the vilest talk about cats.

    Ideally, you should choose a male with the sensibilities of Da Vinci, who is said to have bought caged animals in the public market only to set them free. Such a man is not afraid to be owned by a cat, but men like Leonardo aren't easy to find. So your safest choice will be a female, not that all of them are perfect for adoption.

Generally speaking, female humans are kind and gentle. But those attributes can become noxious liabilities if the woman you adopt is too needy. If you are her only true friend, she will depend on you to dispel her loneliness, and you'll have no time to call your own. She'll swoop down on you in the middle of your bath or smother you with kisses when you're sound asleep.

Similarly, the female who prefers cats to children may focus her latent maternal instincts on you. Having special treats and an endless assortment of toys is all right, but being dressed in little outfits is an indignity no cat should have to suffer. This kind of woman will never leave you alone for more than a few hours. If she works, she'll come home for lunch just to check on you, and you'll have no peace in your life. On short errands, she may even carry you with her in a little pouch slung over her shoulder, with just your whiskers sticking out.

If your adoptee has a group of her female friends over, you'll end up smelling of a dozen different kinds of powders and perfumes. The scents will be so strong you may have trouble enjoying your favorite food or locating your litter box. Then, should you have an accident on the carpeting, you'll be rushed to the veterinarian for a confidential chat about your toilet habits.

I mention these drawbacks because you should understand that the human you adopt, male or female, will never be perfect. In the best of circumstances, you'll have to put up with behavior that you find objectionable or downright silly. Even so, the advantages of having a human of your own usually outweigh the disadvantages, if you pick wisely.

Another factor to consider in the adoption process is the age of your human. Unless you're prepared to cope with boundless, aimless energy, the very young make poor adoptees. The mediation of older humans (a mother or father, for instance) can make life with an immature human more tolerable, but even then you should expect to be carried around like a rag-doll, petted harder than you like, and followed into your most secret hideaways.

Human children have been known to barber and even paint the cats in their homes. Few things are more ridiculous than a red-green-yellow feline with bald patches pursued by toddlers intent on tying a ribbon to his tail.

The very elderly are sometimes your best choice. Despite health problems and failing memory, they will rarely forget you. Arthritis can't stop them from keeping your litter box clean, and cat food is always at the top of their grocery list. In some instances, you will become as important to your elderly adoptee as his own children. Perhaps you will even find yourself in his will as the principal heir.

The final and most complicated element to consider when ascertaining what type of human you are considering is disposition. The range runs from calm to hyperactive and from positive to pitch-black negative, with a long distribution between each extreme. In some cases, humans veer wildly from exuberance to suicidal depression, which makes them unpredictable and more difficult to manage.

Because disposition is not linked in any way with color, gender, or age, the adoptive cat must, in the end, rely on intuition. A human who presents himself as jovial on the day he is adopted may quickly turn blue and brood for weeks. There is no way to guard against this deceptive aspect of human nature, so each adoption presents an unsettling element of chance.

By nature, we felines don't like surprises. The more one day is like the previous one, the easier we can cope. Adopting a human with a volatile disposition will guarantee instability, so do your absolute best to avoid the frazzled life.

B. More Than One Human 🐾

In many instances, the human types I've described can be adopted in pairs or even in small groups. Oddly, having more than one human in the house doesn't increase the likelihood of trouble. In fact, the opposite is true. The chances of adopting two humans with exactly the same disposition are statistically remote. Typically, one human counteracts the other in a variety of ways, and a kind of harmony is achieved in the household.

This doesn't mean that all is bliss. Couples sometimes disagree and even separate, but as a rule the two person adoption works well. Even more surprising is the multi-human house. Anywhere from three to five people can easily be managed by a single cat. If one human becomes angry or depressed, the others usually intercede and soon restore the old order and the collective disposition of the place.

Of course, common sense dictates a limit on the number of people any one cat should adopt, though I've done quite well with my bookstore staff and all the store's patrons. I think the saving thing for me is the time I have alone overnight. I can sniff out some of the volumes in the new book section or give myself a languid bath. By the time the doors open the next morning, I'm ready once more for my managerial role.

Whatever the number of humans in a household, a cat can choose how available he wants to make himself. If you're the sociable kind, you'll probably interact with everyone, but if you're introverted you may feel more at ease selecting one person for special favors such as lap-sitting and petting. In some cases, a cat can snub everyone and show interest in humans only at meal-time. It's remarkable how readily humans accept this kind of behavior. Some even take pride in the cat's independence and privately identify with him the way adolescent humans admire and emulate their more popular friends.

A household that includes your adopted human and another who doesn't like cats can make your life less than ideal. This awkward situation arises when humans (usually females) allow themselves to be adopted even though they know that their human partner doesn't want to be owned by a cat. Sometimes the not-a-cat-person comes onto the scene after you've lived happily with your chosen human for years. The tension in such a home may last for weeks or even months and have a detrimental effect on your quality of life.

As the feline in dispute, you have no choice but to become a catalyst for change. More often than you might imagine, the reluctant human can be won over through persistent lobbying by your adoptee. As she wheedles, you can best assist her by turning the cat-hater's stereotypes to your advantage.

Exaggerate your sweet, needy side (if you're female) or break out the machismo (if you're male). The simplest gender-stereotyped ploys are best: Let him find you sleeping next to him (atop the covers, down by his feet) or raise your hackles and howl through the window as though fending off zombies.

In some obstinate cases, your only choice is to widen the rift between the humans. Because your adoptee already believes (with justification) that no good person can dislike cats, you must bring out the worst in the one you've failed to convert. Some amount of trickery is fair, such as deliberately running between his feet and screeching as though you've been booted. While he sleeps, you can cover his clothes with your hair. In the morning, you can let him catch you gnawing his toothbrush.

When the breaking point arrives, you will be alone with your adoptee, and she will thank you for helping her see how she was wasting her time with such a brute. On those rare occasions when your adoptee is male and the heretic female, the same tactics can be employed with comparable results.

C. Human Children 🐾

As noted earlier, children can complicate a cat's life. If they are young enough to be carried around by the scruff of their necks (so to speak), you must keep a respectful distance. Any direct interaction with infants may cause even your adoptee to worry about the harm you might cause. If a baby starts to cry while you're close enough to be accused of mischief, you will invariably be blamed. And heaven help you if an adult finds you curled up alongside a sleeping baby.

For reasons that even we cats don't fully understand, humans believe us capable of injuring or even suffocating small children. This superstitious fear extends to the most devoted adoptee, so you should never assume that anyone will give you latitude where a baby is concerned.

Unfortunately, the best course of action is not simply to stay far away from small children, because your distance will be interpreted by humans as dislike or even disdain of their young ones. You must create opportunities for your adoptee to show you to her children. Typically, she  will hold you while drawing near enough for the baby to see you clearly and touch you. If his touch is more punch than pat, you can score innumerable points by pretending you didn't notice. To hiss or strike back is to guarantee your banishment.

Interacting with older children is less complicated, especially if your adult adoptee is raising them properly. However, if she has allowed you to adopt her only to use you as a learning tool for her offspring, you will find it in your best interest to adopt at least one of the children as soon as you can. Nothing is worse than being a child's daily duty if he doesn't feel close to you. Feeding you, refreshing your bowl of water, and even scooping your litter box will seem like chores to him, and he will likely neglect these essential tasks if adult supervision lags.

Most children who have advanced beyond their wild kitten stage can be won over and adopted by using the tactic of intense attention. Even more so than adult humans, children of the species believe themselves to be the center of the cosmos. You can use this to your advantage by contributing to the delusion. Spend all your available time with the child of your choice. Even go so far as to follow him around the house, pretending interest in everything he does. Eventually, he will allow you to adopt him, believing all the while that you have acknowledged him as the pinnacle life form.

D. Other Creatures in the Family

Sensing their need for contact with other species, humans surround themselves with a variety of animals. While we cats prefer a cat-only household, we often find ourselves in a menagerie of dogs, parrots, goldfish, turtles, hamsters, ferrets, and other cats. Pythons, skunks, and even the occasional chimpanzee aren't as unusual as you may think.

The cat who is in the market for a human can always detect the zoo-smell emanating from an over-enthusiastic collector of pets. I scent them out in the bookstore on a daily basis, sometimes picking up musk that I can't identify, wondering if it might be ocelot or ostrich.

Although a species-diverse household reflects a big heart and an open mind, no cat needs the tension of living with a snake or the temptation of a canary. However, if you're the adventurous type, keen for the exotic rather than the dependability of the everyday, you may find yourself drawn to such a home. The life of the wrangler isn't for me, but I understand that some cats love it and manage their assorted housemates without serious incidents (though now and then, I hear, a gerbil disappears).

Of course, you're more likely to encounter dogs and other cats when your adopted human takes you home. Dogs are rarely a serious problem, including brutish mastiffs and nervous little poodles. In most instances, you can adopt them, too, after a period of adjustment. And in the worst cases, you can make it clear that you are best left alone. Just extend your claws and swing for the nose.

Other cats present a more difficult problem. Because they have adopted the same human and have lived in her house long enough to establish territories and a routine they all accept, a newcomer disrupts what is sometimes a fragile truce. The process of your assimilation may take months and is directly affected by the number of other cats in the house and by the temperament of each.

Naturally, you will want to mark territory of your own, but the scent of other felines will be everywhere. Though you'll be tempted to spray, think of spraying as the nuclear weapon in your arsenal. Once used, it poisons the environment and is likely to cause a response in kind from the other cats. The best approach is the persistent use of your

chin and mouth on doorways, furniture legs, and even your adoptee's shoes.

Over time, your personal scent will blend with every other cat's, and you will jointly own both your human and every square foot of her house. This doesn't mean that you will be intimate friends with the other cats, simply that you will become party to a new truce. Should you strike up a close relationship with one or more of your fellow felines, you will be amazed how pleased your adoptee will be and how much more she will dote on those who cuddle and pile together. This in itself is incentive enough to get along.

Whatever your domestic situation regarding type and number of humans and the presence of other creatures, certain kinds of human behavior remain consistent. Primary among them is the human tendency to anthropomorphize the other living beings around them. You may be talked to like a human child or taken into your adoptee's confidence as if you were a human equal.

Some cats find this behavior objectionable because they feel it demeans them, but most accept it and think of it as a harmless eccentricity. Personally, I'm amused when someone looks down at me and asks, "Read any good books lately, little guy?" Though the question could be regarded as condescending, it's better to accept it as an attempt at cross-species communication (however inept).

Whether or not you like it, your human will give you a name. It may be as plain as Bob or as pretentious as Rachmaninoff. Even worse, those names will be varied, through affection and the human's desire for camaraderie, to Bobby, Bobbo, Roberto, Rocky, Manny, Noffy, or altered to Buster, Boo-Boo, Furball, or something sillier yet.

No doubt, humans feel that trying to relate to us on their own terms is a compliment. In their world, humans are considered superior. In ours, of course, there's a different hierarchy.

Chapter 2
Some Common Misconceptions About Humans

To err is human; to purr, feline.

The feline association with humans can be traced back thousands of years, and both our species are believed to have originated on the African continent. The ancient Egyptians held us in such high regard that the penalty for killing a cat (even accidentally) was death.

Many of the books I've read in the store contend that cats in the ancient world attained the status of gods. Why this contention is always made with a tone of amazement is a mystery to me, especially as we hold a very similar place in contemporary society. Surely, we are no less adored than were our ancestors among the pyramids, and it's no exaggeration to say that many humans worship us today.

Imagine archaeologists two thousand years from now digging in the ruins of what used to be a great city. They won't find any mummified felines, but our image will be everywhere—in tapestry, carving, jewelry, ceramics, and bits of clothing. Looking back from such a great distance in time, those future students of human history may rightly conclude that we cats held a privileged, perhaps even godlike, place in the lives of devoted people.

Despite our long association with humans, or maybe because of it, we felines sometimes believe the worst about people. A huge black cat who rummages in the alley behind the store tells me through the basement window that all humans are alike, and he doesn't mean in a good way. I suppose his view is based on bad personal experiences, but I'm sure he's also the victim of broadly held notions that must be set aside if a cat hopes for a successful adoption.

In the remainder of this chapter, I will address a few of the common misconceptions about humans so that the adoptive feline can approach his selection with a more open mind.

A. Humans Are Untrainable

There's no point in denying that humans can be obstinate and set in their ways. If you're a cat wandering the neighborhoods in search of the right home, you can prove this simple truth through observation. Night after night, inside lighted windows, humans ignore good advice from friends and relatives and disregard their own common sense. You can see them making bad choices for their health, their finances, and their relationships.

Because catnip is our worst indulgence, it's difficult to understand human excesses. So it's no wonder that we sometimes question human intelligence. No other creature on the planet knowingly poisons its own body or risks everything for a momentary rush of adrenaline. Still, it is a mistake to assume that humans cannot be trained to behave in ways that suit an adoptive cat.

Take as an example the kind of human who keeps no regular schedule for his own meals and tends to forget yours. Because a bit of pizza crust at midnight is a diet no cat prefers, it's necessary to condition your adoptee to your feeding regimen even if he neglects his own. The two basic approaches are the aggressive and the passive.

If you choose the aggressive ploy, you will want to nose your way into as many food items as you can find in the house. Tearing open a bag of potato chips at 3 A.M. will bring your adoptee wide awake, but it may not be enough to get your message across. You must engage in sustained foraging—jumping inside the refrigerator each time he opens the door, tipping over the bottle of milk left unattended on the counter, even playing with uncooked macaroni shells from the box you chew your way into.

As you pretend to be obsessively interested in anything remotely edible, it's important to initiate a pattern of demanding food. This means setting up a yowl at various times during the day, but particularly in the very early morning and late afternoon. If your adoptee is asleep, let your cries of hunger awaken him. If he's padding about the house in his boxers and paying you no attention, follow him while making a prolonged cry.

Even the densest human will eventually discover that you can be kept quiet if you are fed regularly. Occasional or sporadic feeding won't do, which is why you must continue howling at specific times until you get the schedule you prefer.

The second tactic is the passive one, and it requires a certain amount of acting ability. If your human isn't feeding you the way you want, you can often get his attention by pretending a complete lack of appetite. When he offers you a pinch of bread, simply turn away. If he plies you the next morning with a saucer of milk, act as if you don't know what it is.

Ironically, the less interest you show in eating, the more inclined your human will be to offer you a variety of foods. If you work this strategy well enough, you will succeed not only in developing a meal schedule but also in getting precisely the kind of fare you like the most.

B. Humans Are Entirely Self-Centered

Technically, this category doesn't qualify as a misconception, because it is true that humans regard themselves as superior to all other creatures. This makes them more than a little self-centered and occasionally condescending, but it also leads them to question their own significance.

Keep in mind how lonely and boring it can be at the top of the food chain. It's not easy being God's primary creation or the culmination of several million years of evolution. Either way, humans have inherited the burdensome awareness of how far they fall short of perfection. At heart, the whole species is insecure, which means human arrogance is a hollow bluff.

Once you see through the bluster, you can manipulate your human in ways that are beneficial to his mental and emotional health. The best treatment for those afflicted with a particular sense of superiority is aloofness. Never sit on a lap or tolerate more than a few strokes of petting. Spend your non-sleeping time sitting alone, perfectly still. While holding this posture, you can close your eyes, stare into emptiness, or look directly at your human. The object in any case is to give the impression that you know something (such as the meaning of life or the true significance of death) as, indeed, you do.

Keeping your distance and your meditative composure will irritate those humans foolish enough to think they should be able to hold you whenever it pleases them. Some may even expect you to come when called, which no cat ever does except for mercenary reasons. In most instances, your human will eventually grow to see that life is all about you, not him, and his acceptance of that new world order will actually give him pleasure.

This phenomenon has much to do with the fact that each human knows how little he knows. Stumped by life's biggest questions, the sensible human is unconsciously eager to give up his spot at the top of the pyramid of beings. When a cat makes it plain that he has understanding and insight that surpasses human comprehension, most humans will defer to the feline. This, of course, is the beginning of the kind of adoration that led in ancient times to deification.

C. Humans Are High Maintenance 🐾

Most humans are self-sufficient and perfectly able to take care of themselves. Even so, stories of needy and demanding people abound and are important to address, if only to dispel the fear that adopting a human means undertaking a life of endless responsibilities.

Typically, your adopted human understands that your exclusive duties include eating, sleeping, and occasional lap-sitting. If you find yourself drawn to a person who has different expectations, you should be aware that complications may arise.

Unless you are by nature or inclination a working cat, it is best not to adopt a human who intends to use you as a mouser. While springing after a mouse is an irresistible impulse, actually catching the rodent is not for every cat. First, there's the disease-carrier factor to consider. (Mice and rats are not known for their good hygiene.) And then there's the taste, which I'm told is a bit like mildewed flannel. But since there's no accounting for taste, you may be among those felines who actually enjoy the tang of capture.

It's important to understand, however, that the human who sets you to hunting expects you to be a killer. Catching your prey and then releasing it so you can catch it again, and doing this repeatedly until the creature is woozy from running and wet with your saliva, will displease your human. So if you are not prepared to kill what you catch, you should avoid the life of the working cat.

Conversely, the human who expects you to eat, nap, and purr may be appalled if you nab a mouse in the kitchen and then bring it to her as a demonstration of your prowess. If she reacts by running away from you or climbing atop a chair or table, you should not follow her with your gift still wriggling between your teeth. And if she attempts to make you drop your prize or take it from you, it's best to cooperate, even if she lets the mouse escape and its quick movement pulls you once more into the chase.

As with hunting, unless you find yourself predisposed to the lifestyle, you should avoid any human who expresses a wish to put you on display.

Some humans impose their desire for beauty and recognition onto the cats who adopt them, entering them in a repetitive cycle of pet shows. Those of you who are purebreds are at greater risk for this kind of neediness, but even we domestic shorthairs are sometimes combed and curried and placed atop a little box in the middle of an arena.

On the surface, this doesn't seem like a bad deal. You get an extraordinary amount of attention and are admired by complete strangers, even if you don't win a ribbon. Underneath, though, the whole affair is as tawdry as a circus sideshow, and all but the dullest purebreds end up feeling exploited.

I know of a tabby with unusual markings who so despised being evaluated for his brightness of eye and the sheen of his coat that he bit a judge. His bad behavior got him disqualified from the show and convinced his human that future appearances were too risky to undertake. Of course, his bold action might have landed him back in the shelter, where he would have been obliged to begin anew the search for a compatible human.

Apart from specific expectations associated with hunting and modeling, some humans have an emotional or psychological need that can be equally oppressive. This type is distinguishable by its behavior when it comes around to be considered for adoption. The primary signs are extravagant kissing—of the head and face and often of individual paws and your "pwecious liddle tummy"—and excessive hugging.

While we all expect the undivided attention of our humans, we want it on our terms. The emotionally needy are likely to invade your space and your privacy whenever they want a "furry fix" and will often become sullen or even lapse into depression when you assert your independence.

Although as a feline you are incapable of feeling guilt or assuming responsibility, having a human with the blues can be a serious downer, diminishing the quality of your life and making you wish you had chosen more wisely. Unfortunately, it isn't always easy to distinguish normal enthusiasm from inappropriate need at the point of adoption.

D. Humans Are Intolerant 🐾

Because most humans are adaptable to new situations, few cats will find themselves living with people who deliberately attempt to change feline behavior. The few exceptions to this rule are sometimes generalized to make the false claim that humans as a species are so demanding and obnoxious that they make it almost impossible for a cat to be himself.

Among these exceptions is the human who establishes house rules that include the cat. It's one thing to ask children to take off their muddy shoes at the door, but it's another sardine altogether to expect a cat to stay off the furniture or the kitchen counter.

Human attempts to impose discipline on a feline can usually be resisted with success, albeit after a period of frustration for both parties. The cat should regard continued scolding and physical intervention (such as his removal from a pile of laundry warm from the dryer or the top shelf of a china cabinet) as a violation of his feline civil liberties. Any cat treated in such a manner is well within his rights to return again and again to any spot the human regards as off-limits.

In the worst-case situations, the intolerant rule-maker may shoot you with a water-pistol or even confine you in a carrier or kennel. Naturally, you should respond to such indignities in the most vigorous ways possible, including yowling, scratching, and biting.

Never, under any circumstances, should you alter your behavior to suit the human. Complying with rules will produce a simmering resentment that will make it difficult for you to interact with your human in more than the most perfunctory ways. Worst of all, permitting yourself to be controlled by your adopted human can lead to terrible feelings of inadequacy and failure.

The most flagrant intolerance is found in those humans who inexplicably don't like felines. While some cats are attracted to the challenges represented by this type of adoptee, the relationship almost never works out to the satisfaction of either party.

The reluctant human typically makes himself available for adoption through abrupt changes within his family. The death of a relative or even a close friend can prompt a wish to fill the void of loss by connecting with the feline left behind. Also, the human may feel obliged to perform a final act of kindness.

Usually, such a person is already known to the cat, at least casually, which makes it hard for the cat to turn him away. At the beginning, the relationship may be helped along by mutual good intentions, but very few of these circumstantial arrangements work out. Being ignored is only marginally better than being criticized for every stray hair or scratched surface. Eventually, separation is the only way to end the unhappy tension of a goodwill stalemate.

Chapter 3
The Habits of Humans

Cats learn more in one year than people learn in seven.

While no two cats are exactly alike, we resemble one another in the way we live our lives. We prefer a dependable schedule, particularly for meals, and can be counted on to follow the same routine each day. Humans are similarly habitual, though their behavior varies much more widely than ours.

In the most orderly household, your human will go to bed and get up at the same time each day. He will eat, bathe, play games, and come and go on a regular schedule. Although his choice

of hours may not suit you precisely, you will do well to try to match your routine to his. The small sacrifices you make—eating at six instead of four in the morning and trying not to romp during his sleeping hours—will pay dividends in the long-run. Disrupting this type of human will invariably lead to disruptions in your own routine, and it's better to have a dependable life even if all its aspects aren't of your choosing.

Unfortunately, not all humans have such regular lives. Many vary their sleeping and eating times so widely that only a kitten can tolerate the uncertainties.

Research shows that younger adult humans are the least reliable when it comes to taking care of themselves. They sometimes stay up well into your own nocturnal hours, often ignoring

you and disrupting your secretive prowling, and they have been known to eat cold soup from a can or skip meals entirely. Not surprisingly, a slipshod approach to their own nutritional needs frequently translates into negligence of your food and water dishes.

Training this kind of human is exceedingly difficult, and his erratic behavior may persist for decades, well beyond our typical life expectancy. Consequently, we don't have time to wait for the maturation process to resolve all the problems and sometimes have no choice but to demonstrate our dissatisfaction by misbehaving in some of the ways previously mentioned.

Most humans fall between these extremes, having schedules that are reasonably regular and habits that vary only at wide intervals. Most cats find it relatively easy to extract small adjustments from these humans to better accommodate the feline life. However, big changes can sometimes be made, and some cats are able to alter their human's daily pattern in significant (even exceptional) ways.

I know of one orange tabby who was so persistent in pushing his morning meal to an earlier and earlier hour that he eventually created an additional meal for himself. Tired of losing sleep and of not knowing when he would be purred or head-butted awake on any particular night, the adopted human instituted a 2:30 feeding every morning. This was in addition to the meals he served regularly at 7:00 A.M. and 5:00 P.M.

A. The Curious Human Work Impulse 🐾

Most humans have jobs. Some refer to their job as their career, but the terminology doesn't change the basic reality for us cats. Simply put, your human will be gone from home for extended periods to do something for which he receives money.

I witness this phenomenon daily as bookstore workers perform tedious, repetitive tasks. Everyone from the man who pushes the vacuum cleaner after hours to the woman who issues memos to the rest of the staff is involved in an activity that seems much less rewarding than a languorous tongue-bath in a puddle of sunlight.

The work impulse is so strong among humans that they often assume I am a fellow participant in their labors. I've been referred to as the store's "official greeter," just because I sometimes sit close to the entrance; the "resident mouser" (as if I cared about the occasional rodent); and even as the "supervisor."

Although humans mean well when they say such things, I couldn't care less about the daily chores that keep the store running. If I have a job (and I feel no obligation to claim one), it's being a cat. I'm not working for anyone, and my payment is what all cats expect—ample food, cozy corners, undivided attention when we want it, and blissful solitude when we wish to be left alone.

The kinds of jobs people perform range from those requiring a shovel to those that can be done with a ballpoint pen. Each kind may have a different impact on the life of the cat, which makes it useful to learn what kind of work your human does before adopting him.

Living with a poultry inspector, for instance, will keep your feline senses in a state of constant alert. No matter how often you tell yourself to remain calm, the scent of chicken will override your control, and you will spend all your time sniffing knuckles and fingertips and dirty laundry. You can say to yourself, "There's no chicken here," but that won't stop you from making that silly scent grimace when the vomeronasal organ kicks in.

Even less pungent jobs give themselves away through scent. The police officer smells of sloshed coffee, the fireman of firehouse soups and stews, the teacher of chalk and pencil lead.

The office computer technician carries with him the fragrance of a dozen perfumes and colognes from those who lean over his shoulder as he works on their machines. The lawyer who plays basketball each noon is a blend of gym floor varnish and yellow highlight marker.

Bombarded as we are by smells, it is wise for any cat to restrict the incoming stimuli by selecting a human who neither offends nor confounds the olfactory system. Adopting a postman is risky enough because he carries the bouquet of a thousand doorsteps; adopting one who likes to sample exotic cheese and wine can drive you to distraction.

Apart from a professional aroma, your human carries with him an attitude connected with his job. Statistics show that most workers dislike what they do to earn money, which means that your chances of adopting a disgruntled human are fairly high. This becomes a problem only if your adoptee sulks at home or pounds the walls in anger and frustration.

Even though they may not be happy in their work, humans usually develop coping strategies that make them tolerable creatures at home. Many seem able to flip a mental switch as soon as they enter the front door—click and the workplace is a darkened room in the back of their mind.

Among the positive aspects of human work are fatigue and weekends. Humans often come home worn out from the physical or mental demands of their jobs, which makes luring them into a recliner or onto a sofa only a small challenge for the cat who wants to replace the warmth of the declining sun with a little body heat.

Weekends also afford opportunities for catnaps, but they are equally good for interacting with your human in ways not available during the work-week. Because humans often treat themselves to special breakfasts on weekends, the resident feline has a chance to sample something other than cereal milk. And the Sunday newspaper spread across the bed is excellent for sharing.

B. The Odd Play Habits of Humans

Some of the things we find amusing are not funny to humans. These include filching a piece of bacon from your human's plate and lying or pouncing on the newspaper while he is reading it.

Although humans refer to us as fastidious animals, we are far less compulsive than our adoptees, who spend days assembling a jigsaw puzzle but can't see how much more fun it is when scattered across the room.

I won't go so far as to say that humans lack a sense of humor, but they tend to take their games too seriously. Just upset a chess board in the middle of a match and you'll find out what I mean. Or disconnect the power cord while your human is trying to reach level seven or nine of some video game, and he will probably weep.

The sad truth is that most human games are so boring the only fun you can have comes from provoking your adoptee. Walking across the computer keyboard, jumbling the draw pile of a deck of cards, and running away with a game-board piece can be minimally entertaining if your human becomes exasperated.

In some instances, you can teach your human to fetch. All you need is a small ball or paper-wad to drop at your human's feet. He will invariably toss it across the room, and all you have to do is show him where it lands by springing over and picking it up. It's important not to take it back to him, no matter how much he calls and signals. If he's a good fetcher, he will come to get it himself and then toss it to another part of the room. All you have to do is continue showing him where it lands, and this game can continue for as long as five to ten minutes, which is four to nine minutes longer than you will find it entertaining.

This is as close as you can come to joining your human in a physical activity. None of the sports he plays will interest you (with the possible exception of billiards), and he knows better than to take you along as his jogging partner.

From your side of the species barrier, it's pointless to try to teach him how to hunt birds and squirrels through the window. He lacks the necessary power of concentration and doesn't have a clue what you mean when you make that soft chattering noise in your throat.

C. The Human Diet 🐾

Every kind of animal and all but the most noxious plants can be part of the human diet. In fact, stones may be the only thing in nature not on the extensive list of human foods.

While an appetite that ranges beyond meat and the occasional nibbling of house plants is difficult to comprehend, you will find it tolerable as long as you don't adopt a vegetarian. Humans who abstain from meat entirely are inclined to be judgmental about your tastes and may even try to convert you to the vegan lifestyle. Because you are a carnivore, a strict diet of vegetables (in whatever form) will diminish the quality of your life as well as your life expectancy.

Cats subjected to meals consisting exclusively of grains and raw vegetables are truly running for their lives when they escape into the neighborhood. If you find yourself in this situation, birds, rodents, and even insects will taste exceptionally good, though your hunting skills may be dulled from too many years of indoor life.

Fortunately, very few humans anthropomorphize us to such an extent that they do us harm. The reasonable human understands that we are not furry little people, even if he sometimes seems

confused about who's in charge. In most households, you will be able to savor the smells and sometimes even sample the fare of the human diet. However, you should never beg for a scrap of anything, not even poached salmon. Insistence is the proper approach to use with humans in the kitchen, though you must take care not to jump directly into the saucepan.

Humans differ greatly in their approach to food preparation. Some take pleasure in elaborate dishes requiring many ingredients. Others are content with macaroni and cheese or canned ravioli. The odds of adopting a gourmet cook are remote, because most humans are in too great a rush to take the time to baste anything for hours or concoct a delicate sauce.

Because they are so often in a hurry, humans (especially the younger ones, as mentioned earlier) tend to eat on the run and have an irregular feeding schedule. Training them to be more dependable in the delivery of your food is among your top priorities. You certainly don't want your human to assume that you can eat whenever he does or go without a meal altogether.

Among the most successful training techniques are excessive yowling in the vicinity of your food and water dishes and chewing on potted plants. The latter is best reserved for the hardest cases, because humans are sometimes slow to make the connection between mayhem and hunger.

D. Human Sleep Patterns

For the most part, humans are diurnal creatures. They sleep (or try to sleep) during the night and remain active throughout the daytime hours. Because we felines are nocturnal by nature, establishing some kind of harmonious living pattern with the humans we adopt can be extremely difficult.

As in the area of diet, younger adult humans tend to keep later hours, which can make them excellent night-time associates. As they grow older and assume more grown-up responsibilities—marriage, children, and careers—they become less companionable during those exhilarating hours of darkness.

Training your human to stay up all night and then sleep during the daytime is possible only if his job requires him to follow such a schedule. Otherwise, your efforts to re-wire your human's brain to appreciate the feline rhythm of life will be wasted. And even if you adopt a night-time worker, you should remember that he won't be around to entertain you between sundown and sunrise. Still, some cats feel that having such a human available for daytime sleeping more than offsets his absence at night.

Although foreign to us, sleep disorders are common among humans. They range from difficulty falling asleep or staying asleep throughout the night to life-threatening apnea. While humans may worry about the length or the quality of their sleep, whatever problems they have usually translate into more nocturnal interaction with us.

The insomniac human typically seeks out the company of his feline owner, creating ideal opportunities for us to be petted, admired, and taken further into the confidence of our adoptees (if we choose to pay attention).

The strangest thing about human sleep is the goal humans set for themselves of approximately eight hours each night. This is a good ten hours less than we typically sleep, though we rarely go under as deeply as the humans we adopt. The soundness of their sleep accounts for much of their crankiness when awakened in the middle of the night and even when the alarm goes off at the hour they selected.

For the rest of the day after rising, many humans remain sleepy; but we cats are wakeful even when we seem to be completely under. The human stress associated with lack of sleep would be eliminated if humans could model their behavior after ours and live lives of wakeful sleep rather than sleepy wakefulness.

Chapter 4
Human Habitats

Home is where the cat hair is.

Apart from shop cats like me, who live at the businesses managed by their humans, felines usually share space with their adopted humans in a house or apartment.

The size of the space can vary greatly, as can the location, but the cat who adopts a human through a pet shop or animal shelter will have no way of knowing the particulars of his new home until he gets there. Ordinarily, the total square-footage of the dwelling matters little, unless the available space is occupied by too many others (humans, dogs, or additional cats).

    I've read newspaper accounts of homes with as many as sixty cats, and the story is always the same. The adopted human can't meet the expectations of so many owners, and they vie among themselves for attention and territory. The result is a kind of domestic chaos to which no cat should be subjected.

    This sad situation is the product of good intentions that arise from a misunderstanding of the human/cat relationship. In every instance in which dozens of cats occupy the same home, the human believes herself to be in charge. Operating from this erroneous belief, she says "Yes" to every cat who offers to adopt her, not realizing that she is being misleading and ultimately unkind.

    Unfortunately, it is difficult to distinguish the serial do-gooder from the ordinary human who is already owned by several cats and suffers the delusion that he is in control when he stops by the shelter "just to take a look." Certainly, no cat ever knowingly selects a human with a home so overrun by felines that training the human must be set aside in the interest of survival and the preservation of some small quotient of feline dignity.

While there is no ideal number of cats per household, there is a limit to the number of us who can be cared for in the ways we require. The human to whom I have conveyed the material in this book (the writer with the yellow legal tablet in the bookstore) is owned by six cats, as is his wife. Together, they easily meet the expectations of their felines, though they are probably unaware of how much time they devote each day to the needs and demands of their owners.

In some homes, one cat may be an excessive number, as in the case of an adopted human who travels regularly and depends on friends and neighbors to fill in for him. Although I've heard of cats who like the single life and don't object to the hit-and-miss attention of sitters, most of us prefer owning a non-feral human who is present for at least part of each day. The training process is adversely affected by absence, which leads to living conditions most felines consider less than ideal.

Ironically, there is no relationship between the size of a human dwelling and its orderliness. Smaller places should be easier to keep tidy and clean, but the tiniest efficiency apartments are sometimes filled with stacks of old newspapers, magazines, pizza boxes, and Chinese carry-out cartons (not always completely empty). The little sink may overflow with unwashed dishes, and the human's dirty laundry may be scattered everywhere, with items of clothing lying where they were taken off.

This kind of irresponsibility is of no concern to the feline unless it includes your care. If you are no more consequential than the unemptied garbage can beneath the sink, then you have not adopted wisely. In the midst of the worst kind of slovenly living, your human should always see that you are fed and that your litter box is kept clean. Nothing else matters, not even your footprints in the dust that covers every surface.

At the opposite end of the housekeeping spectrum is the human who vacuums and dusts compulsively, bends to pick up the tiniest pieces of lint, and maintains a level of order and cleanliness seldom seen outside a hospital operating room. If you find yourself living with this kind of person, you are most likely a Sphynx, because you have sensed that your hairlessness suits his lifestyle. With no fur or whiskers to deposit on the furniture or carpeting, you find it easy to fit in.

If you are a more typical domestic shorthair who rashly adopts such a neatness fanatic, you may find yourself wishing for the filthy efficiency apartment. Your human's endless fretting will make you nervous, which will cause you to shed even more than usual, thereby provoking more fretting, which will unsettle your stomach and cause excessive regurgitation of food and furballs, leading to still more fretting by your human, then to heightened nervousness for you, and . . . . The cycle usually ends in separation or feline neurosis, occasionally both.

To be fair, I should point out that most humans fall short of these extremes and are moderately conscientious about keeping their (and your) home in a livable condition.

The typical human cleans his living space on an irregular schedule or when he expects friends or family to visit. For this kind of human, any hair you shed is no more consequential than the dustballs that gather beneath the bed and sofa.

A. Urban Dwellings 🐾

Adopting humans in cities becomes easier each year because we are so well suited to apartment living. Unlike dogs, we require no outdoor exercise, nor does anyone have to follow us around with a scooper and plastic bag.

In the smallest apartments, humans do not need to be trained to leave interior doors open, because there are none. The cat can command the entire space from a single position on the back of a sleeper-sofa, and his human is never out of view. This kind of accommodation eliminates one of the most frequent points of contention between humans and cats by making nothing off-limits. Larger loft apartments often have the same interior openness and offer additional room to romp and scat.

One- and two-bedroom apartments are frequently shared, because of the expense, which doubles and sometimes triples the cat's ownership responsibilities. These spaces also introduce the annoyance of closed doors.

At the top of the list of the advantages of city living is the food. When properly trained, your human will occasionally stop by the butcher-shop to buy a half-pound of liver just for you. Better still, the city dwelling human frequently dines out (at higher quality restaurants than his suburban counterparts) and brings home extraordinary leftovers like lobster, braised lamb, and strawberries topped with Devonshire cream. You can easily train your human that the sensible way to share is to give you generous portions of the seafood and meat and most of the cream (keeping the fruit for himself).

The greatest risk in apartment living is open windows (with or without balconies). The view from thirty stories can be mesmerizing, even if it offers only the rooftops of smaller buildings and other apartment windows across the way. And though we're known for our exceptional balance, we felines sometimes turn the wrong way for maximum sunlight or spontaneously lunge at a lethargic pigeon, forgetting how precarious our perch is.

I've read of cats falling great distances from upper level apartments and surviving with only minor injuries. The record height for this phenomenon is 45 stories. Unfortunately, this is the exceptional outcome, because landing on your feet is not much different than landing on your head after you've reached a certain velocity. Consequently, you must train your human to keep the windows closed or to open them only enough to let a breeze blow through. The only way to do this is to scare your human by sitting on the ledge of any window he leaves open. A little deliberate risk can save your life if it convinces your human that he is responsible for preventing high-level accidents.

B. Suburban Homes 🐾

Suburban adoptions are probably the most common, as more people live on the outskirts of cities than in their centers. Also, the term "suburban" includes neighborhoods that develop around medium-sized and smaller towns.

The primary difference in the suburban home is space. The interiors are larger than those of most apartments, and single-family houses always come with a yard, where your humans will spend part of their time in good weather.

The presence of the yard presents an inside/outside option that isn't available to felines in the city, where only feral cats spend any appreciable time outdoors. City cats who choose the life of trashcans and alleys do so because they have adopted intolerable humans, and those who live life on the streets without choosing it are either lost or abandoned.

In suburbia, however, you may feel the urge to explore the outside world simply because it is so near and enticing. You can see it through multiple windows, and several doors lead directly into it. Getting there through speed and deception is relatively easy, but it isn't hard to persuade your human that you need to be put out each night to fulfill your true calling as a cat.

It's impossible to say this without sounding insulting, but humans are stunningly naïve about the cats who own them. They compare us to our larger cousins in the wild and conclude that we need to hunt (despite the fact that we are fed regularly and are rarely hungry) and to mark territory (which we manage quite adequately indoors).

So, in defiance of local ordinances and common sense, many humans open the door each evening to a world of danger for felines who are (let's face it) not prepared to cope with a wild onion let alone cars and stray dogs. I'm perfectly willing to admit that I don't know how to cross a busy street or what to do in the presence of a raccoon.

Facing up to our limitations as domestic creatures, we must train our humans to keep us indoors. Though it is difficult for most of us, expressing interest in the outside world only through a window and declining opportunities to step outside will usually put an end to open door offers. Should your human forcibly put you out, you can break him of the habit by staying immediately outside the door, scratching and howling to be let back in.

C. Life in the Country

Adopting a human who lives on a farm is not advisable if you want to live exclusively indoors.

Few farm cats are able to persuade their humans that they have no place among the rest of the livestock. While this doesn't mean that you will be relegated to the barn or stable, it is likely that you will spend at least part of your time there.

Humans who choose the rural life often have a different attitude toward cats. Unlike their urban and suburban counterparts, these humans are not usually inclined to pamper the felines who try to adopt them. It's not that they don't care but that they regard most animals as self-sufficient.

If you live on a farm, you almost certainly did not come from a shelter or a pet store. In fact, it's likely that you were dumped by some inconsiderate humans and then wandered onto the farm and took up residence, probably with many other felines who were already there. You know your human is big-hearted because he sometimes sloshes milk into a shallow pan and laughs as all of you rush up to drink. But you know, too, that anyone who raises animals for slaughter is unlikely to be sentimental.

The bargain you make with such a human is one of partial attachment. He is never entirely owned by you, and you are never part of his livestock operation. The benefits for each of you are purely intrinsic. He takes pleasure in running a hand down your back as he passes by on his way to some chore, and you have the chance to spend time with animals of other species. In reality, you adopt the farm rather than the farmer.

Of course, farm life can be dangerous, and for reasons more subtle than hooves and machinery. Because farmers rarely take the time to have their barnlot cats neutered, feline populations expand to the point at which some natural epidemic reduces their numbers. The farmer tends to think of it as nature's way, and if his attitude seems cold or even cruel, then you should pass up every farm until you reach a small town with cozy houses and well-kept lawns.

D. The Vagabond Life 🐾

I've read of a cat who travels cross-country by motorbike with his human. I've even seen a photo of him, a tabby in goggles staring out from a fur-lined saddlebag. How pleased he looks to be roaring down the highways of America. And what a perfect match they are, the burly, tattooed man and his adventurous feline.

But the more typical itinerant humans are less colorful. They range from long-haul truckers, who provide a home on eighteen wheels, to hobos who think of an empty warehouse by the railroad tracks as a four-star accommodation.

As with farmers, these humans are not for every cat. You must be temperamentally suited to perpetual traveling and, in some situations, to a life of hardship.

What you get in return is the constant devotion of your human, who will feed you even when there's barely enough food for himself and can't imagine life without you. He will pamper you to the best of his abilities and take you to places few cats ever see.

Even the homeless are suitable for adoption by the right kind of feline. Living in a cardboard box underneath a bridge won't suit if you prefer a queen-sized bed with a big quilt. But sitting in the lap of your human near a campfire made of foraged twigs, both of you listening to the river whisper past, can be rewarding. Think of it as life stripped of all pretensions, a return to the way things once were for both human and cat. If you have the right disposition, you may find this arrangement more appealing than a penthouse.

Chapter 5
Human Grooming and Toilet Habits

Modesty is a human trait mysterious to cats.

Few humans are as fastidious as we are, though most of them take relatively good care of their appearance. Vanity and social pressure ensure that minimal standards of cleanliness will be met, though human fashion sometimes permits an unkempt presentation. Ripped jeans, tattered sweatshirts, and a three-day's growth of beard for men are not uncommon in public.

While we cats are sometimes fitted by our humans with collars and little identity tags, humans themselves go much further. They routinely pierce various parts of their bodies with gold and silver adornments and wear bracelets and necklaces (variations on the collar) as well as rings. For some, precious metals and stones are signs of wealth; for others they are a statement of individuality. Despite their best efforts, however, humans cannot avoid looking remarkably alike.

The prevalence of tattoos among humans may indicate their unconscious desire to be marked in the interesting ways we felines often are. Human skin in its plain condition varies little, except for gradations of darkness. In a famous, long-running Broadway play, humans went so far as to paint their faces and wear imitation feline outfits. The effect was amusing, albeit more than a little insulting—rather like blackface in Vaudeville.

A. Bathing

Most humans spend a fraction of each day immersed in water or standing beneath an artificial downpour. This makes them essentially self-cleaning, even though they never get the same sheen that the rough edge of a feline tongue gives.

Like us, humans sometimes bathe together, particularly during the early period of a relationship. As the years pass, the frequency of such mutual grooming declines until it finally ceases entirely. The obvious explanation for this phenomenon is the connection humans make between bathing and sex, an association that is entirely missing among us felines.

Whether bathing solo or in tandem, humans employ a variety of soaps and scents, bubbles and oils. As a rule, these additives pose no risks for feline health, although drinking more than a few laps of soapy water has been known to cause some felines intestinal distress.

You may find it amusing to entertain your human by sitting on the edge of the tub to swat the rising bubbles or to fish for his fingers beneath the water. The danger of slipping over the edge is slight, but if you do fall in you will pay for your clumsiness by spending the rest of the day drying out and grooming yourself.

B. Grooming and Dressing 🐾

After bathing, many humans apply scents to themselves that may interfere with your ability to pick up the more subtle smells you are accustomed to reading in your environment. Female humans are more inclined than males to employ lotions, perfumes, and powders; and the intricacies of their grooming rituals offer chances for you to have some fun. Tiny brushes, sponges, and pencils are excellent toys that you can swat around, carry underneath a bed, or hide in some other place for the diversion of your human, who will be entertained first by searching for the missing item and then by retrieving it.

The male human may find it amusing while shaving to place a dollop of lather on the tip of your nose or to encourage you to stick your paw into a foamy bit plopped onto the edge of the sink. Cats seldom fall for this practical joke more than once, though the dripping faucet is something we simply cannot train ourselves to ignore.

Despite the small amount of hair on their bodies, humans daily employ brushes and combs and can be trained to set aside a special implement for your grooming. Although human combing of your fur is no substitute for your own bathing, many cats find it pleasant. Being immersed in water is unpleasant and undignified and any self-respecting cat will resist it.

You must take care not to let your human go too far in applying his hygienic tools to your care. It's fun to watch him brush his teeth and then listen to him gargle, but you will not enjoy having your own teeth scrubbed with a special brush bought just for you. Should your human try to introduce this practice into your life, a vigorous (borderline violent) resistance will usually persuade him to desist.

Before your human leaves for work each day, he chooses clothing from at least one closet and various drawers. For the male, the process always includes the same items—underwear, socks, shirt, slacks, jacket, and shoes. These parts are largely interchangeable, which means that he requires little time to dress.

For the female, dressing each morning is a process of elimination. Skirts or slacks are matched with various blouses, vests, and scarves and cast aside according to the whim of the moment. Selecting the right jewelry to wear involves considering not only the colors of the clothing she eventually chooses but also the level of formality she feels is necessary and even the season of the year. Choosing the proper pair of shoes can lengthen the entire process considerably.

Unless he rips the seat of his pants while getting into the car, the male will rarely return to alter his wardrobe for the day. But the female frequently changes her mind even after she is backing down the driveway.

These differences have little effect on the feline, although they give rise to the age-old question concerning which is more cat-like, the male or female human. The argument in favor of the male typically focuses on his nonchalance, his assumption that he looks good without a lot of fuss. Cats who feel the female embodies more of their traits point to her meticulous attention to details that give her a kind of feline mystique.

Once dressed, male and female usually try to avoid picking up any more of your hair than is already attached to their clothing. They may even use a sticky roller device to remove hair and lint or wipe down their garments with a moist cloth. You should not be offended by this procedure and may even show that you harbor no hard feelings by rubbing against trouser legs and sleeves as your human passes near on his way out the door.

C. Reflections on Mirrors 🐾

Humans spend a surprising amount of time each day in front of mirrors. The male studies his face while shaving; the female while applying makeup. Both use the mirror when brushing their teeth and flossing and to make a final check of their clothing before leaving the apartment or house.

Apart from these practical uses of mirrors, humans also privately assess themselves when only we cats are around to notice. They consider their bodies in full profile, often pulling in their stomachs, or attempt to glimpse their own backsides. Sometimes they even regard themselves completely naked, striking poses that would embarrass them if someone played them back later on videotape.

Humans seem to need the reassurance of mirrors or the confirmation they offer that things could be better. We cats are interested in our own reflections only during the early stages of kittenhood, when we are naïve enough to think what we're seeing is actually another kitten.

Humans have various theories about why we ignore ourselves in mirrors, the prevailing one being that reflections emit no scent and are therefore of no interest to us. The truth is we have such an acute sense of how our own bodies displace the surrounding air that a mirror image is inferior information.

If you want to give your human something to think about, make eye contact with him in a mirror and then turn to look directly at him, indicating that you know the difference. This small, ordinary demonstration will make you the subject of many conversations, and you'll be regarded as special.

D. Toilet Habits 🐾

Humans are curious creatures when it comes to toilet behavior. They are almost uniformly able to take care of their own needs, but the privacy most require is irritating to the typical feline. No matter how many times we demonstrate in our own litter boxes that bodily functions are nothing to be embarrassed about, humans still tend to lock themselves away and show their displeasure if we come mewing at the door.

They often supply their toilet areas with magazines and books to distance themselves from the process they're engaged in, as if it were something unnatural. While we cover our deposits with litter, humans cover theirs with a lid and then flush them away with gallons of water. Afterwards, they often mist the area with air freshener, which does nothing to improve the air quality.

Although humans don't like to think of themselves in animal terms, we cats know that the male of the species retains vestigial traits of marking territory. A free-ranging tomcat roams a wider territory when he sprays, but the male human rivals him within the limited space of the bathroom.

The ongoing tension between male and female humans regarding the position of the toilet seat is directly connected to the male's unconscious need to assert his territorial rights. Each time he leaves the seat up, he signals his most recent claim to the toilet area.

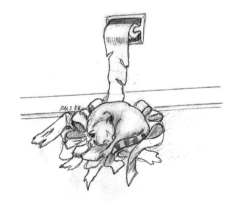

In some households, the female human is able, through tireless effort, to train her male companion to observe bathroom habits that are almost as considerate as ours. If the male who agrees to sit each time he visits the bathroom feels a bit emasculated, I can only say, "It could be much worse."

Chapter 6
Human Mating Habits

For the cat love is not an emotion but a state of being.

The natural impulse of all living things is to continue the species. If you are, as the humans say, an "unfixed" cat, whether in the country or the city, the urgency to procreate is central to your daily life. The same cannot be said for most domestic cats, who must accept neutering as a requirement for human adoption.

No cat who keeps all of his or her reproductive organs can fit comfortably into the world of humans. In fact, ownership of a person will always

be secondary to the hormonal pressures you feel. These will drive you to behave much more aggressively than you might wish and can even cause you to abandon the domestic life altogether in search of mating partners.

Neutering is a pact we make with humans in the interest of getting along. Of course, you may from time to time feel the same vague emptiness that childless humans experience. But when you consider the massive number of homeless, starving cats and humans, you can't help but conclude that having offspring is a selfish act that worsens the problem of overpopulation.

Unfortunately, humans find it difficult to reach this plateau of philosophical vision in their own lives. Most pair off and have children, and the resulting changes affect your life in significant ways. Babies always detract from the attention you are accustomed to receiving, and some humans become so devoted to their newest addition that they will allow it to take your place entirely. In such instances, you will be handed along to a friend or family member or returned to the shelter to begin the adoption process anew.

In the world of felines, sex is not a recreational choice; it's a serious matter of fulfilling our genetic destiny. Whether or not either party enjoys it is not the issue. For humans, though, sex is regarded as an intimate pastime, and men and women engage in liaisons that have nothing to do with the production of children. For them, it's fun, though it often causes them nothing but problems.

A. Sex and the Single Man

As the owner of a human, you are in a unique position to observe a species that has turned mating into a recreational activity. If your human is a single man, there's a strong possibility that he offered himself up for adoption because he intended to use you to attract women. As with almost everything else in his life, sex is the primary motivator. It absorbs most of his waking thoughts and unsettles his dreams at night.

It's likely that he considered adopting a dog, thinking he could take it out for walks and conveniently meet women who stopped to ask what kind it was or to pet it. Nothing cuts through the formalities of an introduction on a sidewalk faster than an exuberant terrier or a slobbering Labrador. Consequently, many single men take on the responsibilities of owning a dog rather than the honor of being owned by a cat.

Your male human, however, obviously thought deeper and realized that although a dog can speed up contact in public, a cat lingers at home as an inducement for women to come over. He probably has photos of you posted around his office cubicle and charms female employees who gather at the coffee pot with stories of your antics. He knows it's just a matter of time until you hook one for his consideration.

If being used in this way offends you, then you're not taking full advantage of the situation. Few creatures are more awkward than the male human on a mission for sex. Having the opportunity to watch him make an utter fool of himself can more than offset your indignation at having been employed in such a calculated manner.

Patience and sex are mutually exclusive for the typical man, which puts him at an immediate disadvantage with most women, who equate fast moves with karate rather than love. Unless he is unusually adept, the single man never understands this difference in perception. He may prepare for an evening of casual touring, but at some point he accelerates to make up for lost time, and that's when he discovers he's not the one who is actually driving.

The most gratifying dates are those on which you get more attention than your manipulative male human. You can facilitate this outcome by sitting on the woman's lap or on the sofa immediately behind her. Most women welcome your diversionary tactics and incorporate them into their moves and counter-moves.

The worst thing your male human can do is to toss you onto the floor or lock you in another room. Naturally, this is exactly the behavior you hope to provoke, because it will destroy the mood for the female and prompt her to leave. This kind of payback for the man who uses you as a lure in his sexual games is sweet for you and instructive for your human.

B. Sex and the Single Woman 🐾

The human female is interested in sex and even enjoys it with the right companion, but sex is not the foremost thing on her mind. When she offers herself for adoption, she is looking for companionship and has no ulterior motives where you are concerned.

Unlike the male human, the female is more open with her emotions and unafraid to say the word "love." She will tell you she loves you and truly mean it. You matter to her because of who you are, and she regards you as a distinct being with a unique personality. This attitude is not unknown among the males of the species, though it occurs naturally in the female without any coaxing or training.

Regrettably, the same capacity for love that makes the female human an ideal adoptee also sets her up for disappointment in her relationships with men. More than sex, she wants affection and devotion, and her gentler desires come into immediate conflict with the male's more carnal ambitions.

Seeing her unfulfilled and repeatedly disappointed, you may decide to help shorten her misery whenever you can by interacting with the men who visit. Sometimes, all you need to do is jump onto the man's lap. If he instantly dumps you or holds up both hands in a sign of surrender as though he's afraid to touch you, your adoptee will definitely abbreviate the evening.

The craftier male knows that by being kind to you he can score points with the woman he desperately hopes to seduce. But half-hearted petting and the constant brushing away of your hair from his jacket and pants will land him at the front door rather than the door to the bedroom.

With very little effort, you can train your female adoptee to regard you as a character detector. Because she's looking for someone with an embracing heart, she will quickly understand that such a man will genuinely like cats. By giving her a dependable standard of measurement for each man who enters her life, you can teach her how to make the best use of her time and spare her the regret of making bad decisions.

Among the benefits you will reap are generous samplings from the meals she prepares for various men who never make it to the dinner table. Over time, you can even train her to fix the dishes you most prefer, in view of the likelihood that you will end up as her dinner companion. Though she may be a little sad to close the door behind one more disappointing man, she will come to regard you as the ideal date.

C. Men and Women Together 🐾

Whether your adoptee is male or female, it's likely that you will have the chance to observe a naked couple doing what comes naturally (though their behavior will only vaguely resemble things you have seen in nature).

Without the modesty of fur, a man and woman in bed together are more anatomical than animal—all skin and knobby joints—connected first at the mouth and then entwined in ways that no self-respecting cats would attempt.

The duration of these encounters varies, with the most active part rarely extending beyond the time it takes you to check your food and water dishes to see if they need replenishing. When the moments of panting and moaning are over, you can easily train your human and his or her partner to lavish you with special attention as they lie together with the sheet pulled up.

If the outcome is pleasant for them, you will be a welcome participant in the good feelings. And if things end awkwardly, you can provide a convenient deflection of attention. Under no circumstances, however, should you expect to be regarded as anything other than a nuisance during the act itself.

D. The Human Dilemma

Sex ranks a close second to hunger on the list of human urges. Like hunger, it can be sated with fast food or a gourmet meal, but only temporarily. To bridge the gap between meals, snacking is commonplace for most humans, and it's fair to say that humans as a group are no longer able to distinguish between what they need and what they want. This confusion often leads to poor judgment at the table and in the bedroom and can express itself in erratic behavior such as binging or abstinence.

While the appetite is keenest in younger humans, it remains active into the later years of human life and reflects a fundamental change in human behavior over the span of our own domestication (at least as long as 8000 years). Few humans these days consciously eat to live but instead live to eat. Similarly, they no longer have sex exclusively to perpetuate life but live to perpetuate sex.

If humans are complicated, it is because their fundamental urges have become confused. In us felines, they find the model of contentment that is lacking in their own lives. But even though they envy the simplicity of our days, which consist primarily of naps and meals, they have so far proved untrainable in this area.

Chapter 7
Some Common Human Ailments

A sick human seeks sympathy; a sick cat solitude.

The human animal is subject to a great number of diseases and disorders, ranging from the common cold and cancer to mild depression and psychosis. Although human ailments are rarely communicable to cats, even the mildest illness can profoundly affect the cat's life.

Few humans are as stoic as we felines. Rather than suffer in silence, the typical human seeks sympathy almost as vigorously as he seeks a remedy for his problem. Consequently, when your human doesn't feel well, he is likely to become even more self-centered than usual and may neglect his duties where you are concerned.

At the same time he is letting your litter box go unattended and altering your feeding schedule according to the fluctuations of his aches and temperature, he will expect more attention from you. Lying beneath a quilt on the sofa or propped up in his bed, your human will want the consolation of your company.

Although you will rightly feel that he has done nothing to deserve it, you can accumulate debts by playing nurse. Also, apart from the annoying coughing and sneezing (in the case of a cold), you can enjoy what is likely to be a new or altered napping spot that includes your human.

Recent studies show that our company improves the lives of our humans by lowering stress and blood pressure. So the human wish to have us near during times of illness may indicate an unconscious awareness that we are good for the overall health of our adoptees.

Some humans believe we have additional healing powers, particularly in the alleviation of pain (headaches, backaches, and post-surgical) and the mending of broken bones. In both instances, our purring is cited as the curative factor. With pain, the rhythmic calmness of our purr is believed to reduce tension and turn down the volume of the brain's pain receptors. In the case of a broken bone, our purr is said to have ultrasonic properties that speed the healing process.

Health-care workers have discovered that we have strongly beneficial effects on elderly humans in nursing homes, especially those suffering from Alzheimer's.

Researchers say that we connect with these particular humans through touch and sound, stirring memory and emotion and thereby enriching lives that have become almost empty. The truth, of course, is that the elderly have attained enough wisdom to recognize that all cats possess ancient souls and therefore make excellent companions in the dwindling days.

A. Diseases That Are Not Species Specific 🐾

Humans are sometimes afflicted with the same problems that affect us cats. Arthritis is common to both our species and causes us similar pain and difficulty with mobility. Likewise, we're both susceptible to various malignancies and share a common prognosis if the cancer is advanced or affects certain vital organs.

Diabetes is more common among cats than most humans realize and requires the administration of insulin to keep it under control. Oddly, a human with the same disease is not necessarily a good choice for adoption. If he is inconsistent in the regulation of his own blood sugar, he will likely be negligent of yours. And the only way you can train him to be more responsible is to let him see the ill effects of his poor treatment. Again, though, if he ignores them in himself, he will probably ignore them in you, putting both of you at grave risk.

Heart and kidney problems resemble one another across the species boundary, although humans have access to surgical procedures that have not yet been perfected for us felines. For example, even though kidney failure is common among older cats, we have no access to dialysis or transplants. The best we can hope for is subcutaneous fluid injections, and I know of one cat named Rosebud Sueann who was sustained humanely for over two years with the daily administration of fluids beneath her skin, living to be twenty-two.

In rare instances, we may share certain diseases with humans that originate with us. Ringworm is one of the most common and is difficult to eradicate without persistent treatment of all cats

and humans infected with the fungus. Although no cat would deliberately pass ringworm to his adopted human, sharing a common irritation can afford an excellent chance for your human to identify with you. Think of it as the "walk a mile in my itchy skin" kind of empathy.

Other cross-species diseases that originate with felines bear mentioning only to underscore their rarity. Rabies, roundworm, and toxoplasmosis are virtually nonexistent among domestic housecats, though they can be found in feral cats and in other cats who are allowed to roam freely. A human who voices concern about any of these diseases is either paranoid or the victim of anti-feline propaganda. Adoption of such a person is usually impossible and always undesirable.

B. Bad Habits 🐾

Because humans are prone to addiction, they sometimes develop habits that are detrimental to their health. Primary among them are smoking and drinking, with the two frequently combined in daily rituals that appear celebratory in the company of other humans but are distinctly morose when indulged in alone.

The harmful effects of second-hand smoke have been well documented among humans, but the cat spends much of his time at floor-level, below the rising smoke, and may be at less risk. In the absence of research into the effects of tobacco smoke on felines, many smokers take the precaution of smoking outside, sometimes tapping on the window as their cat looks out.

Although excessive drinking by humans has no directly harmful effects on felines, the consumption of large amounts of alcohol presents risks to the resident cat. Heightened levels of inebriation lead to irresponsible and sometimes even rash behavior—phoning in an obscene job resignation, making a threat against the mayor or the president, smashing objects ranging from dishes to televisions and pianos. Even if the chaos is only momentary, it can be very traumatic for the cat of the house.

As with smoking, training your human to quit drinking is a hopeless undertaking. No matter how many glasses of vodka, gin, bourbon, or scotch you knock over, he will always have a refill. Even worse, he will incorporate you into his nightly ritual, stroking you as he sips his drink. As pleasant as this may seem, it puts you in the same category as beer nuts or potato chips, and no cat wants to be a side dish.

C. Serious Substance Abuse

Marijuana is the most common substance of choice for humans who choose to move beyond tobacco and alcohol. The second-hand effects of marijuana smoke are presumed to be as harmful as those associated with tobacco. And the problem is worsened by the fact that many marijuana users also smoke cigarettes.

Humans who try to share their marijuana with cats through second-hand contact are wasting their weed and their breath. No cat needs to have his doors of perception thrown open or his attitude adjusted. The best a human who uses marijuana can hope for is a poor approximation of the sense of wholeness we felines possess naturally.

The closest we felines can come to understanding the attractions of marijuana is in the appeal of catnip. Like cannabis, it is a naturally occurring plant whose leaves, buds, and blossoms alter behavior. While catnip has no discernible effect on humans, it causes most of us cats to respond in distinct ways after sniffing, rubbing against, or ingesting it. Humans often describe our reaction to the weed as a "kitty high," and they frequently make the substance available more for their amusement than for our satisfaction.

Among the harder drugs used by humans, methamphetamine is by far the most prevalent. It produces increased activity and a general sense of well being, but as its effects wear off the user becomes agitated and sometimes violent. The meth addict is like a young cat chasing his own tail. The faster he goes, the faster his tail races away. No amount of acceleration will produce a different result, so the objective of the activity is largely the activity itself, with the goal always being inexplicable and unattainable.

Among the other highly addictive drugs used by a significant percentage of humans are various prescription medications and cocaine. Whatever the substance, the human adoptee who is under the control of his addiction cannot respond fully to your efforts to care for and train him. Even worse, the addicted human will almost certainly mistreat you through neglect. Without professional help, the addict will steadily destroy himself and the life you hoped to share when you adopted him.

The odds of your adopting a human with a profound drug problem are relatively small. It's much more likely that your human will be addicted to something harmless, like chocolate or caffeine; so don't be put off adoption because of the extreme examples which are cited here to afford a sense of the full range of human addictions.

D. Mental and Emotional Health Issues

By far, the most common mental health problem for humans is depression. It may manifest itself as chronic despondency or as an acute sense that life is meaningless and day to day living pointless.

As the owner of a human suffering from this kind of existential anguish, you are likely to be the first and sometimes the only one to know. Depressives are good at covering up when in the company of other humans, and they often reserve their bleakest moments to share with you.

Naturally, no cat feels lucky to be the confidante of a human who sighs rather than breathes and lugs himself around his house or apartment as if his body were a burden to carry. At his worst, the depressive human finds only a glum solace in your company and may even come to envy or resent you for your steady temperament and obvious satisfaction with life.

Professional therapy can be helpful, as can certain kinds of prescription drugs, but nothing is more available and meaningful than the life affirming attitude you embody. Consequently, your best course of action is to be yourself and hope that your human will eventually become more like you.

The more serious kinds of mental and emotional disorders usually prevent the humans who suffer them from entering the adoption process. This means that the psychotic and the seriously neurotic human are rarely available for consideration by any cat. While this works out well for us felines, it deprives some of the most profoundly troubled humans the benefits of our guidance.

Mental disorders for the average human have little effect on his ability to function normally and tend to your needs. If your adoptee compulsively checks and re-checks the doors each night to be sure they're locked, he is not certifiably mad. If he returns home immediately after leaving for work to be sure he turned off the coffee pot, he is more normal than abnormal. These types of behavior are best labeled eccentricities rather than defects, particularly as they have no negative implications for the feline of the house.

Chapter 8
Human Aging and Dying

No one dies wishing he had petted his cat less.

The average human lifespan exceeds eighty years, but it's an oddity for a cat to live into his twenties. Statistically, this means that your human will almost certainly outlive you, leaving him orphaned and available for another cat to adopt.

During his lifetime, a human can expect to enjoy the companionship of many cats, but each cat anticipates owning only one human (or one family). This makes the selection process all the more important for the feline, who can't afford to choose a person who will make his less-than-twenty-years unpleasant.

Of course, statistics never tell the full story, nor do they include all the likely possibilities. Instead, they straighten the road and make their conclusions seem like inevitable destinations. In the actual living of life, one finds many detours and byways.

Accidents and illnesses sometimes end human lives prematurely, leaving the cat in the statistically remote outpost of survivor. Few cats in this situation regard themselves as lucky. Unlike our human charges, we felines are so fully engaged in each moment of living that our own death is of no concern to us. However, the death of a loved human is a traumatic blow no cat is prepared to suffer.

The sudden removal of a cat's human is as significant as the obliteration of the sun. One of the constants he relied on is gone. Because no cat likes even minor changes in his daily life, the death of an adopted human can cause confusion and uncharacteristic behavior. Humans say such a cat is depressed or bereft, but it's more accurate to describe him as dispossessed. His routine and his familiar home have vanished with his human. No wonder, then, if he sprays in an effort to redefine his space or refuses to eat or yowls in the middle of the night.

I know of two cats who lost their owners and never adjusted. One was a fairly young cat whose elderly owner died and left instructions for her to be euthanized. Unable to honor that last wish, the relatives gave the cat a chance to adopt a new family, which she did with great reluctance. Although she was accommodated in every way, she never accepted her new home or her new people. For two years, she spent most of her time in hiding, and she eventually died of malignant tumors in her abdomen.

The second cat was an elderly Burmese who was asked to adopt new people when his human of eighteen years entered an assisted care facility that wouldn't allow cats. The separation was very much like a death, and the Burmese lasted only three months before succumbing to a stroke.

In both these cases, the clinical cause of death was, in reality, a physical manifestation of the trauma of losing a human. Neither feline was able to continue living in a world from which the principal point of reference had vanished.

Though these cases are somewhat exceptional, they reveal how difficult it is for us to move on after the loss of our human. The period of adjustment, both to the loss and to a new adoptee, varies greatly from cat to cat. It may take a few weeks or a few months and can be made much less difficult by a human who gives the dispossessed feline the time and space he needs.

A. The Myth of Time 🐾

Humans are controlled by time. They strap it to their wrists, hang it on their walls, and fall asleep with it glowing next to their beds. It is the primary source of human anxiety and occasionally a point of conflict between their species and ours.

Unlike humans, we do not believe in time—at least not in time portioned like a pie into equal pieces. For us, there is but one universal moment that hums in our heads like a purr. It is undifferentiated, continuous, without beginning or end. Consequently, we have no deadlines, no schedules other than those we devise to train our humans to feed us, and no concept of our own mortality. In fact, each of us knows we are as infinite as the moment we inhabit.

Living with a human obliges us to cope with his fiction of time. Of course, we occasionally remind him of the folly of his clocks by waking him in the middle of the night for a snack or luring him into a nap when he meant to be doing something else, but no cat should undertake the complete conversion of his human to feline impulses. Few humans in the history of their species have attained the sense of unity that is known to all us cats.

For the most part, our human's temporal delusions have no effect on us. If we remark his comings and goings at all, they rarely disrupt our seamless lives of browsing at the food dish, staring out the window, and napping. Whatever he writes on his calendar is as inconsequential to us as the difference he perceives between Tuesday and Saturday.

B. Life Expectancy and Mortality 🐾

Because of his obsession with time, the human coverts his own life and the lives of everything around him into days, months, and years. He devises tables and charts to estimate how long he can expect to live, and he imposes his own sense of time onto other species.

According to sources available to me in the bookstore, the average life span for a human now approaches 30,000 days (about 82 years). If your human is typical, he expects to live at least that long, and he unconsciously assumes that he will retain reasonably good physical and mental health into his eighties and beyond.

As he contemplates his own longevity, your human converts your life into his years. To accomplish this, most humans multiply your age by a factor of seven. If you're five, they will log you in at 35. And if you've reached what they consider your average life expectancy of 14 (about 5100 days), they will regard you as being 98. Obviously, a 14-year-old cat isn't the equivalent of a human approaching the century mark, so you can assume this conversion method is seriously flawed.

Although more complex formulas have been devised, resulting in comparative ages that seem more reasonable, all are based on human years and are therefore meaningless to us cats. It makes no difference if my humans at the store consider me to be middle-aged (in human terms) or elderly. I am alive in the enduring moment, and that's all that matters to me or to any other cat.

Mortality is the primary reason humans play these games with numbers. They fear death, and because they want to live as long as possible they are continually seeking ways to extend their lives. Sometimes they focus on diet, sometimes on exercise, and some spend a fortune on vitamins and natural herbs in the hope that they can keep hearing the ticking of the clock.

The most important thing we can try to teach our humans is to bask in life, forgetting the shadow of death. If they, like us, measured only the limitless pleasure of being alive in the world, we could curl up together in a sunlit understanding.

C. Faith and Religion

The ancient Egyptians worshipped dozens of gods and goddesses, including one in the form of a cat (Bastet). In our contemporary world, most humans have winnowed down their pantheon of deities to one (or in human terms, the One) god. Although they know him by different names, he is invariably all-knowing and all-powerful and he is presumed to be male (unlike Bastet, who has the body of a woman and the head of a cat).

It is likely that your human believes in god. His belief may be expressed through some kind of formalized religion or as a personal, unstructured sense that some greater force is at work in the cosmos. However he conceives a higher power, his belief in it will intensify as he grows older and contemplates the nearness of his own death.

Human faith, then, is a composite of uncertainty and fear. We felines have no use for it because we know what we know and are content. Ordinarily, your human's religious beliefs will not intrude into your life, though you may wish you could imbue him with a greater understanding that would put him at ease.

In moments of enlightened reflection, your human may sense that your perception goes much deeper than his. He may stroke you and tell you how he envies your blissful, encompassing soul. He may stare into your eyes as though trying to read your mind, not realizing that in such moments he is very near the ancient worship of Bastet.

D. Body and Soul 🐾

Recently, the manager glimpsed another cat just after the store had closed for the night. I was sitting beneath his desk lamp, so he knew it wasn't me. After searching for half-an-hour, he blamed his imagination, finished his tasks, and left.

What he didn't know was that I had two predecessors in this building before it was remodeled into a bookstore. Wayne and Roger padded through this space at different times many decades ago.

I could have told him this within the first few weeks of my tenure here, because their scent lingers in out-of-the-way places and tells their separate stories. Wayne was an orange tabby. Roger was solid white with ears shortened by frostbite. I know these things because a cat's scent conveys his entire identity.

Since the manager's odd experience, several patrons and a few workers have come forward with stories of ghost cats. One claims to have heard a cat meowing within a locked room but found no evidence of him when she entered and looked around. Another swears that he felt a cat rub against his ankles as he was thumbing through a book but saw nothing when he looked down.

Such human scenting of indelible feline presence is extremely rare, and its authenticity is often obscured by false encounters. Impressionable humans who crave evidence of something that extends beyond the physical have proliferated reports of contact with Wayne and Roger to the extent that all such accounts have lost their credibility.

This is regrettable, because I know for a certainty that Wayne and Roger are still here. They have not changed from the way they were in the past because they were almost pure spirit to begin with (as are all cats). The inability to see them or pet them makes them no less real.

Some day, when everyone thinks I've gone, I will join Wayne and Roger, and the three of us will prowl this building, searching for that singular human who is ready to learn the rest of what we know.

Afterword

If we felines advertised our adoption services the way some businesses tout themselves, we could accurately state that we have been caring for and training humans for over 8,000 years (perhaps as long as 10,000, according to recent archaeological discoveries).

Over the millennia, we have become so expert at human manage-  ment that the humans under our care actually believe themselves to be in control. This belief is so deeply ingrained in them that divulging the truth here will evoke only a chuckle.

During our long association, we felines and our humans have resolved our most difficult problems. Cats have become so accustomed to the litter box that even as kittens we understand its purpose (almost as if it has become genetically imprinted). And humans have retained enough of their ancient admiration for our elegance and poise to allow us to be ourselves, without any notion that we have utilitarian value.

The issues that arise in today's cat and human household are usually small and easily addressed, as this handbook illustrates. The few exceptions (such as an adoptee who insists on imposing his rules on his adoptive feline) occur infrequently and should not dissuade you from adopting a human. In all but a few instances, you can alter your human's behavior to suit you and thereby improve life for you both.

If you are a cat who is scenting out the meaning of this book, you are probably already in charge of a human's home and know well how much the advantages outweigh the drawbacks. Your challenge is to get the word (or scent) to those cats who are wandering the neighborhoods, tentatively thinking about adoption. With a concerted effort, we can increase our total adoptions from the current estimate of 30 percent of all households to at least 50 percent within the next decade.

If you are a human who has not been adopted, you should immediately make yourself available for consideration at the nearest animal shelter. At this very moment, there is at least one cat there, waiting for you.

Made in the USA